ABOUT THE COVER IMAGE

This artwork is the negative image of a heart, painted in textured acrylic on canvas and digitally modified, symbolizing the art of living and leading from the inside out.

Walking

THE

Heart Path

Walking

— THE —

Heart Path

BITE-SIZED BITS OF WISDOM ON
LIVING & LEADING FROM THE INSIDE OUT

DEDICATION

To Michael & Allison
Always & Forever

May you always know that no journey is worth traveling without love, respect, and kindness, no matter how outwardly beautiful it appears to be. No life is worth living if we cannot fully embrace and accept both ourselves and others. There is no success without sacrifice and hard work, and no acclaim worth attaining if we lose ourselves in the process. In the end, the security we seek is not to be found in things, but in the currency of trust, self-respect, Faith, love, and acceptance, from which we can then make our way in the world.

With much love,
Mom

ACKNOWLEDGEMENTS

Without apology or reservation, my journey has been a spiritual one and it is my faith in God above all else that gives meaning and purpose to the road I travel. In a world that often idolizes ego over heart, fear over love, and external 'success' at any cost, the teachings of my own Christian faith and those of other traditions play a central role in my core beliefs, serving as both anchor and compass during those times when I falter and/or struggle to hold onto my own faith and footing.

While the writings and artwork in this book are original to me and derived from personal experience, there are those I wish to acknowledge whose own ideas have influenced my own and whose support along my journey has made all of the difference.

My three-year participation in Lolly Daskal's on-line leadership discussion group, Lead From Within, never failed to inspire, and I thank her and the many heart-based leadership colleagues I've met over the years through this forum and others, many of whom have provided direct support, advice, and/or encouragement along the way, including: Alli Polin, Emelia Sam, Jon Mertz, Simon Harvey, Bill Treasurer, Chip Bell, Mike Henry, Martina McGowan, Samantha Hall, Chantal Bechervaise, Eileeen McDargh, Susan Mazza, Joseph Haslam, David Greer, Becky Robinson, Paula Kiger, Becky Sansbury, Stephanie McDilda, and Paulette Ashlin. Special acknowledgment goes to Jesse

Stoner and S. Chris Edmonds. Thank you both for your steadfast presence, generosity, wisdom, and guidance, and for being among the very first to lead me into this wonderful world of leadership. You truly walk your talk in all that you do, and I am grateful to call you friend.

To those dear friends who from the outset helped push me out of my fear and into my voice, including Kristin Brumm, Gail Summerskill, Lorin Mask, and the brave women of the Afghan Women's Writing Project, I am grateful beyond measure. To my followers, friends, mentors, and colleagues who regularly take the time to read, comment, and cheer me on from the sidelines, including #teamawesome friends Laura Cook, Gesù Antonio Baez, Belinda-Rose Young, and Jaslin Kalsi, thank you for reminding me of why I write and why this work matters.

Special thanks goes to: Stan Phelps (a.k.a. Stan, Stan, the goldfish man) for your humor and endless positive energy, and for holding me accountable to outcomes; to Nancy Olah, for your friendship, legal advice, and belief in my work; and to Grace Watt, for introducing me to the brilliant and heart-led Carmen Barnhill, whose fabulous design work has brought the words on these pages to life. Carmen, you have beautifully captured my vision for this project, and I thank you for your patience with my endless edits!

Thanks, too, to Whitney Johnson, for inviting me to share this piece of my dream with you, for it is in giving voice to our dreams and sharing them with others that we begin to take the steps necessary to finally realize them.

To Matt, I thank you for your friendship, laughter, support, encouragement, and faith in both me and my message. The journey is so much more fun with you in my world!

Heartfelt acknowledgment goes to my parents, whose emphasis on the importance of character and core values helped shape my own, with special thanks to my mom and fellow writer and sister, Linda Perkins, whose unwavering faith, love, and support has made all of the difference.

Finally, I am eternally grateful to my children, Michael and Allison, for encouraging me to write, and for patiently listening to my ramblings and words of (unsolicited) wisdom along the way. You are my constant inspiration for all that I do.

KEY

Each of the symbols below represents core themes that are central to living and leading a heart-aligned life and are provided as a key to help you navigate your own journey though this book.

 THE AUTHENTIC VOICE

 THE ART OF BECOMING

 DREAMING IN FULL BLOOM

 GROWING STRONG

 NAVIGATING CHANGE

 BUILDING RELATIONSHIPS

 LIVING YOUR VALUES

 SERVING ABOVE SELF

 LEADERSHIP

THE
Journey
BEGINS

INTRODUCTION

In early 2009 and beyond, I embarked on a journey *within* that led me away from a life once defined by external labels of worth and success – a journey I call walking the 'Heart Path', and the name under which I first penned my writing. It was during this period of intense personal growth, learning and heightened self-awareness that I also began to awaken and reconnect with my own sense of wonder and creativity, drawing insights from life, love, business, and politics, expressed through my deep passion for words, inspiration, and art.

Along the twisty road, there have been many bumps, trenches and potholes, all of which helped shape my perspective and strengthen my resolve to live and lead an authentic, heart-aligned life. In addition to my own life experience and lessons learned along the way, I have also had the good fortune of guidance and support from those who have walked this path before me, an insatiable appetite for continual learning and growth, combined with a hefty dose of grace and hard work. All of this I collectively refer to as *hard-(l)earned wisdom.*

The quotes in this book reflect many of these insights and the core values with which I try to live my life out loud. As you navigate and walk along your own heart path, my hope is that these bite-sized bits of wisdom challenge you to reflect more deeply on your own life and leadership, inspiring you to dig deeper, dream bigger, and courageously follow your heart – finding peace, love, and joy in the journey itself.

Sharon

PREFACE

Heart-based living and leadership mean many things to many people. For clarity, it is not about sentimentality or abandoning sound reason and logic in your everyday life. Rather, it is about aligning your life and leadership with your core values and learning to lead from within. Embracing the principles of servant leadership, many of the quotes contained in this book emphasize the importance of character and intentionality in a world that is more often focused on the expedient, expendable and convenient. While the values I touch on are universal in nature, they are nevertheless influenced by my own Christian faith; the insights reflecting an honest account of my own imperfect walk.

IT ALL STARTS WITH
THE HEART.
♡

HEART-ALIGNED LIVING &
LEADERSHIP IS INTENTIONAL,
MINDFUL & DELIBERATE. ROOTED IN
AUTHENTICITY, IT REQUIRES FIERCE
COURAGE, LIMITLESS FAITH & A
DEGREE OF VULNERABILITY THAT
CHALLENGES US TO STEP OUTSIDE
OF OUR COMFORT ZONE & INTO THE
WORLD OF GROWTH & POSSIBILITY.
IT REQUIRES INTEGRITY, TOO; THE
ABILITY TO NOT ONLY STAND UP FOR
WHAT'S RIGHT BUT TO STAND IN
THE WHOLE TRUTH OF OUR BEING;
TO FULLY HONOR & ACCEPT OUR
IMPERFECT SELVES, JUST AS WE SEEK
TO ACCEPT OTHERS — WITH LOVE,
GRACE, & COMPASSION.

WHEN WE REACH THE END OF A ROAD,
IT'S TIME TO BLAZE A NEW TRAIL.

WHEN APPROACHED
CONSTRUCTIVELY, CONFLICT CAN
LEAD TO TREMENDOUS GROWTH. IT
TEACHES US ABOUT WHO WE ARE &
WHAT WE VALUE.

IMPOSSIBILITY THINKING COMES
FROM A PLACE OF FEAR & A LACK OF
FAITH. POSSIBILITY THINKING COMES
FROM A PLACE OF LOVE & A
FUNDAMENTAL BELIEF THAT ALL
THINGS WORK TOGETHER FOR GOOD.

PERFECTIONISM IS THE ENEMY OF
PROGRESS. JUST DO IT.

THE BUTTERFLY AWAKENS
TO ITS OWN BEAUTY, JUST
AS ITS WINGS BEGIN TO
UNFOLD, READY TO
TAKE FLIGHT.

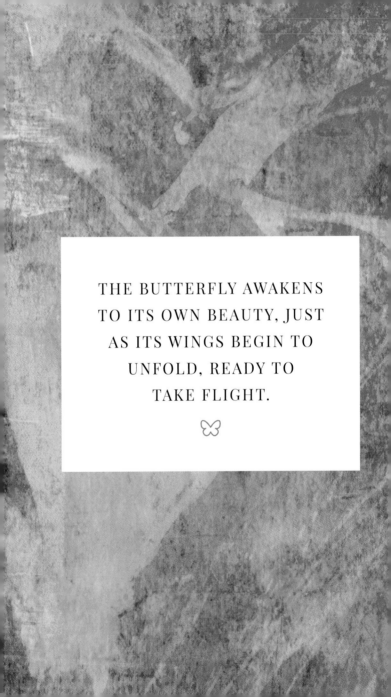

BELIEVE IN THE BEAUTY OF YOUR
DREAMS, FOR THEY ARE THE
SACRED VOICE OF YOUR HEART
& SOUL.

DURING SEASONS OF CHANGE, IT IS
HELPFUL TO REMEMBER THAT GRIEF
IS NEITHER FINITE NOR LINEAR. IT IS
NOT A PLACE FIXED IN TIME, BUT A
PASSING THROUGH.

TAKE TIME TO ACKNOWLEDGE &
APPRECIATE THOSE YOU
JOURNEY WITH.

EXTEND YOUR HEART. OPEN YOUR
MIND. BROADEN YOUR PERSPECTIVE.

Faith is the foundation from which we find the courage to lead & serve.

TO LIVE & LEAD FROM THE HEART,
WE MUST FIRST JOURNEY WITHIN.

SOMETIMES OUR STRUGGLES ARE
NOT FOR OUR BENEFIT, BUT ARE
FOR THE BENEFIT OF INSPIRING &
EMPOWERING OTHERS THROUGH THE
GIFT OF OUR OWN EXAMPLE.

THE TRUE VICTOR IS THE MAN
WHO CAN COMPETE WITHOUT
COMPROMISING HIS INTEGRITY IN
THE PROCESS.

EVERY PATH HAS THE POTENTIAL TO
TEACH US MORE ABOUT OURSELVES.

THE REAL GLORY IS NOT FOUND
IN ACHIEVING OUR OWN AIMS
& AMBITIONS, BUT IN SERVING
OTHERS; FOR IT IS OFTEN THROUGH
SERVICE TO OTHERS THAT WE
FINALLY KNOW OUR TRUE CALLING
& PURPOSE.

IF HOW WE LIVE SHAPES THE
COURSE OF OUR OWN LIVES, HOW WE
LEAD HAS THE POWER TO SHAPE &
INFLUENCE THOSE AROUND US.

THE VALUE OF A PATH CAN BE
MEASURED BY THE SIZE OF ITS
HEART. WHERE THERE IS NO HEART,
THERE IS NO POSSIBILITY FOR JOY.

Values define
the quality of
the journey.

⚖

THE REAL GLORY IS NOT FOUND IN
GOING ALONE, BUT IN WHAT WE CAN
ACHIEVE TOGETHER.

FAR TOO OFTEN, WE SELL OURSELVES
SHORT AND SELL OURSELVES OUT:
WE ACT FROM A PLACE OF FEAR. WE
ACT FROM A PLACE OF PRIDE. OR
SOMETIMES, WE FAIL TO ACT AT ALL.

WE CANNOT CHART A NEW COURSE
WHEN WE'RE STILL SAILING IN A
DIFFERENT DIRECTION.

WHEN WE LIVE A DIVIDED LIFE, WE
OFTEN END UP LOSING THE VERY
ESSENCE OF WHO WE ARE.

HUMILITY IS A POWERFUL,
GROUNDING FORCE, IF WE'LL ALLOW
ITS RIGHTFUL PLACE IN OUR LIVES.
IT IS NOT HAUGHTY OR BOASTFUL
OR PROUD. IT CENTERS & GROUNDS
US IN OUR WISDOM, WHILE GENTLY
REMINDING US OF ALL WE STILL
HAVE TO LEARN. IT DISMANTLES OUR
EGO, WHILE OPENING OUR HEARTS.
IT BUILDS BRIDGES INSTEAD OF
WALLS. IT UNIFIES RATHER THAN
DIVIDES.

SO OFTEN WE SPEAK OF FINDING
OUR CALLINGS WHEN OFTEN OUR
CALLINGS FIND US. WE CAN CHOOSE
TO HONOR OR IGNORE THEM; TO
FIGHT OR EMBRACE THEM. WHEN
WE ALLOW LOVE TO GUIDE OUR
THOUGHTS, WE ARE OPEN TO THEIR
GIFT; WHEN WE ALLOW FEAR TO
ARISE & DICTATE OUR DIRECTION,
WE DENY OURSELVES & THE WORLD
THE GIFT OF OUR TRUE SELVES.

WHEN WE WAIT ON THE WORLD
TO GIVE US PERMISSION TO BE
OURSELVES, WE ROB OURSELVES (&
OTHERS) OF OUR OWN TIME, TALENT
& TREASURE.

True empowerment begins with the deep knowing that you matter.

WHEN WE FIND THE
COURAGE TO LIVE OUR
VOICE OUT LOUD, WE NEED
NO LONGER BE AFRAID.
OFTEN OUR GREATEST
ACT OF BETRAYAL IS TO
OURSELVES.

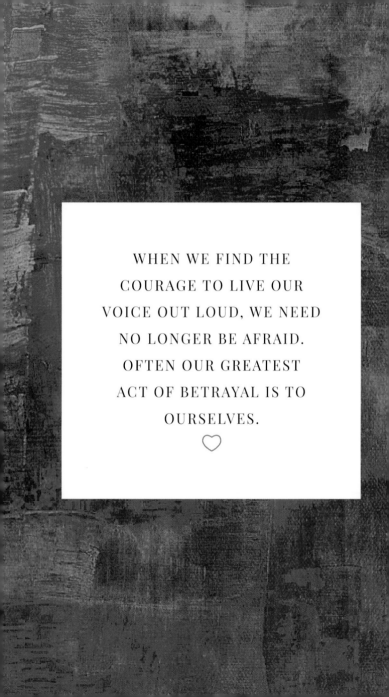

NEVER ALLOW FEAR,
DISAPPOINTMENT, OR DEFEAT TO
DROWN OUT YOUR DREAMS. WHERE
THERE IS A WILL, THERE IS USUALLY
A WAY . . . YOU MUST SIMPLY STAY
OPEN TO THE JOURNEY ITSELF.

WE ARE NOT SUPPOSED TO HAVE
ALL OF THE ANSWERS. PART OF
LIVING A HEART-ALIGNED JOURNEY
IS LEARNING TO EMBRACE THE
QUESTIONS THEMSELVES.

HOPE SAYS, "ANYTHING IS POSSIBLE
IF I AM WILLING TO MOVE FORWARD
IN FAITH & FAITHFULLY WORK
TOWARDS MY DREAM."

WE STEP OUT OF OUR FEAR BY
STEPPING UP OUR FAITH.

THE BEST LEADERS DO NOT NEED
TO SELL YOU. THEY LEAD QUIETLY,
GENEROUSLY & CONSISTENTLY. BY
THE GIFT OF THEIR OWN EXAMPLE,
THEY ATTRACT & EARN A
LOYAL FOLLOWING.

IN EVERY MOMENT WE HAVE THE
POWER TO CHOOSE: TRUTH OVER
FICTION; LOVE OVER HATE; HOPE
OVER DESPAIR.

START SMALL, BUT DREAM BIG.

Serve with a
loving heart.
Love with a
servant's heart.

IF HOW WE ACT WHEN NO ONE IS
LOOKING MOST CLEARLY REVEALS
OUR CHARACTER, THE HONESTY,
TRANSPARENCY & TRUTHFULNESS
WITH WHICH WE CONDUCT OUR
LIVES & RELATIONSHIPS WITH
OTHERS REVEALS THE HEART OF OUR
INTEGRITY. INTEGRITY, AFTER ALL,
IS MORE THAN TRUTH TELLING. AT
THE HEART OF INTEGRITY IS TRUTH
& THE ALIGNMENT OF ACTIONS
WITH OUR STATED VALUES. IT IS THE
'RIGHTNESS' OF OUR BEING, NOT OUR
SELF-RIGHTEOUSNESS.

CHOOSE WISELY, ACT
COURAGEOUSLY, GIVE GENEROUSLY,
FORGIVE EARNESTLY, LOVE DEEPLY.

THE MOMENT WE QUIT DREAMING IS
THE MOMENT WE STOP MANIFESTING
MIRACLES IN OUR OWN LIFE, FOR
WHEN WE HAVE NO INTENTIONAL
AIM, WE MOST ASSUREDLY WILL GET
LOST IN THE WILDERNESS OF LIFE.

OUR REAL STRENGTH AMIDST
CHANGE LIES IN HONORING OUR
DEEPEST SELVES & CONVICTIONS.

YOUR LEADERSHIP GIFT IS YOUR
ESSENCE IN ACTION.

IT IS NEVER TOO LATE TO CHANGE
THE COURSE YOU ARE ON.

SOMETIMES WE MUST SUFFER THE
PAIN OF FALSE MASKS, THAT WE
MIGHT FINALLY LEARN TO WALK
IN THE TRUTH OF WHO WE
AUTHENTICALLY ARE.

THERE IS NO 'LONER' IN LEADERSHIP.
IT TAKES A TEAM APPROACH TO
ADVANCE SUSTAINABLE PROGRESS.

THE BEST TEACHERS IN LIFE ARE
NOT THE ONES WHO PRESUME TO
HAVE ALL OF THE ANSWERS, BUT THE
ONES WHO CAN HELP US FIND
OUR OWN.

OUR HEART HOLDS THE
KEY TO OUR DEEPEST
DREAMS & LONGINGS.

❀

CHOOSE YOUR WORDS WISELY, BUT
LIVE IN SUCH A WAY THAT YOU CAN
ALWAYS SPEAK COURAGEOUSLY FROM
YOUR HEART.

ON THE JOURNEY TO BECOMING OUR
AUTHENTIC SELVES, SOMETIMES
WE WEAR HAND-ME-DOWNS UNTIL
WE'RE COMFORTABLE IN OUR OWN
SKIN. WE MIRROR THE PATTERNS,
BEHAVIORS, & VALUES PASSED DOWN
TO US UNTIL WE FEEL SAFE ENOUGH
TO CHALLENGE THE STATUS QUO.

IN EVERY DARKNESS THERE IS
LIGHT, IN EVERY FAILURE THERE IS
LEARNING, & IN EVERY STRUGGLE
THERE IS THE GIFT OF GROWTH &
INVITATION TO JOURNEY ON.

The capacity to overcome begins with hope, faith, & the fundamental belief that change is possible.

LIFE & THE PROSPECT FOR LASTING LOVE, FRIENDSHIP, JOY, PEACE, & PROGRESS BEGINS THE MOMENT WE'RE WILLING TO ACCEPT RESPONSIBILITY FOR BEING FULLY *'HERE'* IN ALL OF ITS IMPERFECTION INSTEAD OF TRYING TO HOLD ONTO OR HOLD OUT FOR THE ELUSIVE *'THERE.'* IN THE END, THE GRASS IN OUR OWN BACK YARD IS AS GREEN AS WE CHOOSE TO WATER, FEED & CARE FOR IT. THE INSIGHTS WE GAIN THOUGH ADVERSITY ARE ONLY AS HELPFUL AS WE'RE WILLING TO APPLY THEM TO OUR LIVES & HELP PAVE A PATH FORWARD FOR OTHERS.

LEAD WITH CONVICTION. LEAD WITH
TRUTH. LEAD WITH RESPECT. LEAD
WITH LOVE.

BEING A ROLE MODEL COMES WITH
A RESPONSIBILITY TO OURSELVES
& OTHERS; TO CARRY OURSELVES
UPRIGHT, EVEN ON THOSE DAYS
OR IN THOSE MOMENTS WHEN WE
STRUGGLE & SUFFER SETBACKS IN
OUR JOURNEY.

TO KNOW THAT YOU HAVE TOUCHED
A SINGLE LIFE BY A KIND WORD OR
DEED, IS TO HAVE SUCCEEDED.

Letting go is
not the same as
giving up.

WHEN YOUR PASSION IS ALIGNED
WITH YOUR VALUES AND GIFTS, IT IS
ALWAYS THE TRUE PATH.

YOU HAVE ONLY TWO CHOICES:
LIVE THE LIFE OF YOUR DREAMS,
OR DREAM OF THE LIFE YOU WISH
TO LIVE.

THE HEART IS THE VOICE OF OUR
MOST AUTHENTIC SELF. LEARN TO
LIVE, LISTEN, SPEAK AND ACT FROM
YOUR HEART PLACE.

HUMILITY IS THE GREAT LEVELER
BETWEEN PRIDE (EGO) &
LOVE (HEART).

OUR CORE WOUNDS CAN LIMIT OUR
CAPACITY TO REALIZE OUR FULLEST
POTENTIAL UNTIL WE BEGIN TO
UNDERSTAND THAT WITH THE RIGHT
NURTURANCE, THEY CAN ALSO BE
THE WELLSPRING OF INSPIRATION,
GROWTH & ULTIMATELY, OUR GIFT
OF SERVICE TO OTHERS.

WHEN WE ARE WILLING TO EXTEND
TRUST & STAND IN THE TOTAL
TRUTH OF OUR BEING, WE OPEN
THE DOOR TO BUILDING AUTHENTIC
CONNECTION WITH OTHERS.

EMBRACE THE BEAUTY OF THE
MOMENT YOU ARE IN.

Find purpose in all that you do, then serve with an open & thankful heart.

LOVE IN LEADERSHIP COLLABORATES.

FEAR IN LEADERSHIP ISOLATES.

LOVE IN LEADERSHIP BUILDS BRIDGES.

FEAR IN LEADERSHIP BUILDS WALLS.

LOVE IN LEADERSHIP IS PROACTIVE.

FEAR IN LEADERSHIP IS REACTIVE.

LOVE IN LEADERSHIP SAYS,

"I AM HERE TO SERVE OTHERS."

FEAR IN LEADERSHIP SAYS,

"I AM HERE TO SERVE ONLY MYSELF."

LOVE IN LEADERSHIP SAYS,

"I EMPOWER YOU."

FEAR IN LEADERSHIP SAYS,

"I CONTROL YOU."

LOVE IN LEADERSHIP SAYS,

"I AM OPEN TO GROWTH."

FEAR IN LEADERSHIP SAYS,

"I AM AFRAID TO FAIL."

WHEN THE VALUES & ACTIONS OF
MANY ALIGN WITH THE VISION OF
THE WHOLE, JUST ABOUT ANYTHING
BECOMES POSSIBLE.

THE POWER OF ANY COMMUNITY
TO SOLVE COMPLEX PROBLEMS &
INFLUENCE CHANGE, BEGINS & ENDS
WITH RELATIONSHIPS & THE TRUE
SPIRIT OF COLLABORATION.

ASSUMPTIONS ARE THE ENEMY OF
POSSIBILITY THINKING.

TOO OFTEN WE LIMIT, DIMINISH
& DEVALUE OUR PRESENT BY THE
STORIES WE TELL ABOUT OUR PAST.

Never believe
you are too
small to make
a difference.

WE HOLD ON UNTIL WE ARE READY TO
LET GO - PLAIN & SIMPLE. THERE IS NO
LOGIC OR WELL-MEANING ADVICE FROM
OTHERS THAN CAN PUSH US ALONG
THIS CONTINUUM UNTIL WE ARE READY
TO MOVE . . . NO GOING BACK EITHER,
THOUGH UNTIL WE ARE WILLING TO LET
GO, WE WILL MOST ASSUREDLY REMAIN
STUCK. THIS APPLIES AS EQUALLY TO
RELATIONSHIPS & LIFE PASSAGES AS IT
DOES TO ANYTHING ELSE.
BUT LETTING GO DOESN'T HAVE TO
MEAN SETTLING FOR SOMETHING LESS
THAN WE DESIRE AND/OR ARE CAPABLE
OF ACHIEVING. IT DOESN'T MEAN
GIVING IN OR GIVING UP, BUT SIMPLY
LETTING GO FROM A PLACE OF DEEP
FAITH, AS THE NEXT CHAPTER IN OUR
LIVES WAITS EXPECTANTLY IN
THE WINGS.

WHEN WE ARE AT PEACE
WITH & TRUST OUR
CALLINGS, WE FIND THE
CONFIDENCE TO SAY 'NO'
TO THOSE PATHS THAT DO
NOT SUPPORT OUR
TRUE NATURE.

SOMETIMES THE PATH TO
EMPOWERMENT BEGINS WITH THE
COURAGE TO PURSUE A CAUSE
GREATER THAN OURSELVES OR
OUR OWN NEED FOR APPROVAL &
ACCEPTANCE FROM OTHERS.

WE GROW IN PROPORTION TO OUR
CORE BELIEF IN OURSELVES, OUR
WILLINGNESS TO CHALLENGE OUR
OWN ASSUMPTIONS, & OUR OPENNESS
TO CHANGE.

IT IS NOT ENOUGH TO KNOW HOW
TO LEAD. IF WE HOPE TO INFLUENCE
CHANGE, WE MUST BE WILLING TO
LIVE OUR LEADERSHIP EVERY DAY.

ONE OF THE GREAT GIFTS OF THE
JOURNEY IS THE PEOPLE YOU MEET
ALONG THE WAY.

ONE OF THE MOST EMPOWERING &
LIFE-AFFIRMING THINGS WE CAN
DO IS TO GIVE LIFE TO A VOICE &
STAND STRONG IN OUR TRUTH, FOR IN
SHARING OUR STORIES, WE NOT ONLY
EMPOWER OURSELVES, BUT INSPIRE,
EMPOWER & PAVE A PATH FORWARD
FOR OTHERS.

LIVING A LIFE OF SERVICE IS
GRATITUDE IN ACTION. IT IS THE
ULTIMATE EXPRESSION OF THANKS
FOR OUR GIFTS & TALENTS.

It is not enough to know ourselves. We must be willing to live our truths every day.

⚖

STAND STRONG IN THE LIGHT OF
YOUR TRUTH, NOT THE SHADOW OF
YOUR FEAR.

NEVER GIVE UP ON THE BEAUTY
OF YOUR DREAMS.

HOLDING YOURSELF & OTHERS
ACCOUNTABLE IS AN ACT OF
RESPECT, NOT REPRIMAND.

OUR CAPACITY TO SERVE & LEAD
OTHERS, GROWS IN PROPORTION TO
OUR DEGREE OF SELF-AWARENESS
& THE COURAGE TO LIVE OUR LIVES
OUT LOUD.

THE TRUTH IS THAT SOMETIMES,
WE CANNOT KNOW IN THE PRESENT
MOMENT HOW THE PEOPLE WE ARE
SURROUNDED BY WILL INSPIRE OUR
LEARNING...WE CANNOT FORESEE
HOW OUR DAILY STRUGGLES MAY END
UP TRANSFORMATIVE IN NATURE,
PROVIDING US WITH FERTILE GROUND
FOR GROWTH & ENABLING US TO
STEP UP & INTO OUR OWN AUTHENTIC
VOICE & LEADERSHIP.

Patience challenges us to detach from ego-based outcomes, reminding us that we are not 'I,' but 'One.'

ATTITUDE, MORE THAN
CIRCUMSTANCES THEMSELVES,
SHAPES THE LENS THROUGH WHICH
WE SEE THE WORLD & OUR ROLE IN IT.

TRAVEL AS MUCH AS YOU CAN; THERE
IS GREAT BEAUTY IN THE WORLD & ITS
PEOPLE, EVEN AMIDST THE RUBBLE.

OUR TRUE PATH IS NOT SOME
DESTINATION OUTSIDE OF
OURSELVES; IT IS THE HEART-
CENTERED JOURNEY OF THE SOUL.

RESPECTFUL DIALOGUE IS
FOUNDATIONAL TO BUILDING BRIDGES
OF UNDERSTANDING.

LISTENING ENABLES UNDERSTANDING;
UNDERSTANDING ENABLES RESPECT;
RESPECT ENABLES TRUST.

IN A WORLD THAT MEASURES WORTH
FROM WITHOUT, ONE OF THE MOST
COURAGEOUS STEPS WE CAN TAKE IS
TO LIVE & LEAD FROM OUR HEART
IN SUCH A WAY THAT OUR OUTER
CHOICES REFLECT OUR INNER VALUES
& VISION FOR THE FUTURE. THIS IS
THE ESSENCE OF SUCCESS.

IT MATTERS LESS WHAT WE'VE
ACHIEVED IN THE PAST, THAN HOW
WE CHOOSE TO SERVE OTHERS IN THE
PRESENT.

WINNING IS NOT ABOUT PLAYING
IT SAFE. IT'S STEPPING OFF OF THE
BASE OR INTO THE NET; STAYING
OPEN TO OPPORTUNITY & TAKING
CALCULATED RISKS. IT'S ABOUT
STEPPING OUT OF THE KNOWN &
INTO THE UNKNOWN. WINNING IS
BORN OF VISION, CONVICTION,
TENACITY, FAITH, & THE COURAGE
TO ACT INSTEAD OF SIMPLY RE-ACT.
IT'S ABOUT PLAYING BIG, NOT
SMALL. SOMETIMES, WINNING EVEN
DEMANDS THAT WE FIRST LOSE,
PERHAPS MANY TIMES, THOUGH IT
IS OFTEN DURING THESE TIMES WE
DISCOVER THAT WHAT MAY PERHAPS
LOOK LIKE DEFEAT OR FAILURE,
IS ACTUALLY AN OPPORTUNITY TO
DISCOVER, UNCOVER OR RECOVER
OUR GREATEST GIFTS.

THE PROMISE IS NOT THAT WE
WILL BE VOID OF PAIN, HARDSHIP &
BROKEN-HEARTEDNESS, BUT THAT
IN THE BREAKING, WE CAN DISCOVER
THE DEPTHS OF OUR HEART, OUR
SOUL, & OUR VERY HUMANITY.

THE 'BOX' IS FULL OF SELF-LIMITING
BELIEFS & ASSUMPTIONS. WE MUST
CLIMB OUT TO SOAR FROM WITHIN.

THE BEST MEASURE OF OUR
COMMITMENT TO ANY CALLING
OR CAUSE IS NOT FOUND IN THE
IMMEDIACY OF AN ANSWER, BUT
IN OUR WILLINGNESS TO EMBRACE
PATIENCE, EVEN AS WE CONTINUE TO
PUSH FORWARD WITH OUR DREAMS.

AUTHENTICITY IS BORN
FROM A WILLINGNESS TO
GIVE UP THE APPROVAL
OF OTHERS IN EXCHANGE
FOR ACCEPTANCE & LOVE
OF SELF.

♡

WHILE EXTERNAL INFLUENCES MAY
DICTATE MANY OF OUR CHOICES
& EVEN REFLECT OUR VALUES, WE
EACH HAVE BURIED WITHIN OUR
HEART AN UNDENIABLE TRUTH THAT
DRIVES OUR DREAMS, REGARDLESS OF
CIRCUMSTANCES WITHIN OR OUTSIDE
OF OUR CONTROL. IT IS THAT STILL,
SMALL VOICE THAT WON'T TAKE 'NO'
FOR AN ANSWER; THE PART OF US
THAT BELIEVES ANYTHING IS POSSIBLE
IF YOU WANT A DREAM BADLY ENOUGH,
& THAT WILLINGLY EMBRACES THE
INEVITABLE SACRIFICES WE MUST
MAKE TO REALIZE OUR DREAM.

WHEN WE SPEND OUR ENERGY
FOCUSED ON WHAT'S BEING DONE
TO, WE HAVE LITTLE ENERGY LEFT TO
ACTUALLY DO.

IMPOSSIBILITY THINKING COMES
FROM A PLACE OF FEAR & A LACK
OF FAITH. POSSIBILITY THINKING
COMES FROM A PLACE OF LOVE &
A FUNDAMENTAL BELIEF THAT ALL
THINGS WORK TOGETHER FOR GOOD.

CONNECTING & COLLABORATING
AS LEADERS, FOR THE PURPOSE OF
CREATING A BETTER COMMUNITY,
STRENGTHENS EVERYONE.

Every step we take is an act of faith. Every step we take in alignment with our values & ourselves is an act of love.

⚖

ASK COURAGEOUS QUESTIONS.
BE WILLING TO GIVE COURAGEOUS
ANSWERS.

AT THE CORE OF LIVING A HEART-
ALIGNED LIFE IS HOPE: FAITH IN
THE UNSEEN, BELIEF IN WHAT'S
POSSIBLE, & THE COURAGE TO
PURSUE THE DEEPEST DREAMS OF
OUR HEART.

SOMETIMES THE LITTLE THINGS
ARE THE SEEDS OF DREAMS &
CHANGE FRESHLY PLANTED, BUT
WHICH NEVERTHELESS REQUIRE
NURTURING, TIME, & ATTENTION
TO GROW INTO THEIR
FULL POTENTIAL.

WHEN WE LISTEN FROM A PLACE
OF LOVE, WE REFLECTIVELY SEEK
TO UNDERSTAND. WHEN WE LISTEN
FROM A PLACE OF EGO AND FEAR, WE
REACTIVELY SEEK TO JUDGE.

TO DREAM IS TO IMAGINE NOT ONLY
WHAT'S POSSIBLE, BUT TO ENVISION
THE IMPOSSIBLE.

THERE IS NO ACCEPTABLE
COMPROMISE FOR INTEGRITY. IT IS
THE ESSENCE OF EVERYTHING THAT
TRULY MATTERS.

THE REAL BLESSING COMES WHEN
WE ARE NOT ONLY ABLE TO FEEL
GRATEFUL FOR PAST STRUGGLES
& LESSONS, BUT ARE ABLE TO
REMEMBER THE GOOD AMIDST THE
DIFFICULT, TOO. AS WE REMEMBER
THE GOOD, WE INVITE AN OPENING
FOR GRATITUDE, COMPASSION &
FORGIVENESS, ESSENTIAL FOR
MOVING FORWARD & LIVING IN
PEACE & JOY. REMEMBERING
DOESN'T CONDEMN US TO RELIVING
OR REPEATING THE PAST, BUT
ENABLES US TO REWRITE OUR
STORIES, FREEING UP ONCE
NEGATIVE ENERGY & CREATING
SPACES TO FULLY LIVE, LOVE, &
LEAD IN THE PRESENT.

It is not enough
to work towards
our dreams.
We must first
believe them to
be worthy of the
journey itself.

❀

TRUE CONFIDENCE IS NOT BORN OF
THE ILLUSIONS & LABELS OF OUR
EGO, BUT FROM THE QUIET KNOWING
OF OUR HEART.

SO OFTEN WE CLING TO THE
ILLUSIONS OF THE SAFE & FAMILIAR
& THEN WONDER WHY NOTHING
CHANGES. WE ARE CALLED IN ONE
DIRECTION, BUT OFTEN BETRAY THE
LONGINGS OF OUR HEART FOR THE
CRAVINGS OF OUR EGO.

IN THE UNDIVIDED LIFE, WE BEGIN
TO DEFINE SUCCESS, NOT BY THE
STANDARDS OF THE WORLD, BUT BY
THE UNCONDITIONAL ACCEPTANCE
OF OURSELVES & OUR ABILITY TO
LIVE OUR TRUTH OUT LOUD.

CHANGE OCCURS WHEN THE COST
OF COMPLACENCY OR INDECISION
EXCEEDS THE COST OF TAKING
A RISK.

WE BECOME WHAT WE IMAGINE &
BELIEVE IS POSSIBLE. WE MUST
THEREFORE LEARN TO DREAM WITH
OUR HEARTS WIDE OPEN.

DO NOT GIVE THE PAST THE POWER
TO DEFINE YOUR FUTURE.

WE INFLUENCE BEST BY THE VALUES
WITH WHICH WE LIVE OUR LIVES
EVERY DAY.

LIVE YOUR VALUES. VALUE
YOUR LIFE.

INSPIRED VISION IS SO MUCH
LARGER THAN OURSELVES. IT DOES
NOT GROW IN ISOLATION, BUT IN
COMMUNITY WITH OTHERS.

DREAM, REFLECT, & THEN ACT
– WITH RENEWED CLARITY OF
PURPOSE, COMMITMENT, &
DETERMINATION.

ENGAGEMENT IS A FUNCTION OF
SHARED VISION & VALUES, NOT
OBLIGATION.

IN EVERY SITUATION, WE HAVE
THE POWER OF CHOICE: WE CAN
MINDFULLY ACT FROM A PLACE OF
SELF-LOVE OR RECKLESSLY REACT
FROM A PLACE OF FEAR. WE CAN
PRACTICE LEARNED HELPLESSNESS
OR EXERCISE SELF-ASSERTIVENESS.
THOUGH WE CANNOT ALWAYS
PREVENT & ANTICIPATE THE
UNWELCOME IN OUR LIFE, THE
MINDSET OF VICTIM OR VICTOR IS
STILL WITHIN OUR CONTROL.
THIS MINDSET IS AT THE HEART OF
REALIZING OUR FULLEST POTENTIAL,
FOR HOW WE VIEW OURSELVES
SHAPES THE LENS THROUGH WHICH
WE EXPERIENCE THE WORLD.

True confidence
is humble; it is
heart-centered,
not ego-centered.

♡

THIS IS WHAT JOURNEYS &
CROSSROADS ARE ALL ABOUT.
THEY ARE ABOUT SEEKING &
HONORING OUR PERSONAL TRUTHS
& COMMITTING OURSELVES TO
DEVELOPING THE VERY BEST IN
OURSELVES, & IN OTHERS, TOO.
FROM THAT PLACE, THE CHOICES
BECOME CLEARER & THE ONLY
QUESTION WORTH ASKING THAT
REMAINS IS: "DOES THE PATH
BEFORE ME HAVE A HEART?" IF
NO, THEN THE PATH WILL LEAD
NOWHERE WORTH GOING. IF YES,
THEN YOU HAVE FOUND YOUR
TRUE NORTH.

YOU CANNOT LET GO IF YOU ARE
ALWAYS LOOKING BEHIND YOU. YOU
MUST STAY FORWARD-FOCUSED.

ON EVERY JOURNEY TOWARDS A
DREAM, THE PATH IS PAVED WITH
POTHOLES, ROAD BUMPS & DETOURS.

SOMETIMES WE NEED TO BE
CHALLENGED TO FINALLY KNOW OUR
VALUE, STRETCHED TO LEARN OUR
LIMITS, & TESTED TO UNDERSTAND
OUR STRENGTH.

THERE ARE MOMENTS WHEN THE
BETTER PART OF VALOR REQUIRES
HOLDING OUR THOUGHTS, NOT
EXPRESSING THEM.

THE POSSIBILITIES FOR YOUR LIFE
ARE ENDLESS. BELIEVE IN THE
UNBELIEVABLE.

WE ALL HAVE PERSONAL FEARS &
DOUBTS. WE ALL HAVE HOPES &
DREAMS, TOO. THE QUESTION THEN
REMAINS: HOW WILL YOU CHOOSE
TO DIRECT YOUR THOUGHTS & YOUR
CHOICES? WILL YOU LIVE & LEAD
FROM A PLACE OF LOVE OR FOREVER
LIVE IN THE SHADOW OF YOUR FEAR?

WE MAY FIND MEANING VIA OUR
INDIVIDUAL PURPOSE, BUT MEANING
IN LEADERSHIP IS COLLECTIVE
IN NATURE.

IN THE FACE OF
SETBACKS & STRUGGLES,
YOU CAN ALLOW FAILURE
TO DEFINE YOU, OR
ALLOW THE LEARNING
FROM FAILURE TO
REFINE YOU.

A LIFE WELL-LIVED IS A REWARD
UNTO ITSELF.

IN LIFE AS IN CHESS, A WINNING
GAME REQUIRES GOOD STRATEGY, A
SOLID SET UP, CONTINUED FOCUS ON
THE DESIRED OUTCOME, & ABOVE
ALL, PATIENCE.

COLLABORATIVE COMMUNITIES
BEGIN WHERE 'I' & 'YOU' BECOMES
SOMETHING LARGER THAN EITHER
COULD ACHIEVE OR IMAGINE ALONE.
IN THIS INTRICATE WEAVING OF
IDEAS THAT SHIFT FROM 'ME' TO
'WE', A BEAUTIFUL TAPESTRY BEGINS
TO EMERGE.

NEVER GIVE UP. SOMETIMES OUR
SETBACKS, WHETHER A 'NO' OR
CLOSED DOOR, ARE THE VERY
CATALYSTS THAT ULTIMATELY
ENABLE OUR DREAMS TO
COME TRUE.

ONE OF THE MOST PROFOUND
EXPERIENCES WE CAN HAVE IS TO
SUCCESSIVELY LOSE EVERYTHING
WE'RE EXTERNALLY ATTACHED TO.
IT IS PAINFUL TO BE SURE, BUT IN
THIS STRIPPING AWAY; IN THE RAW
VULNERABILITY THAT REMAINS,
WE CAN BEGIN TO KNOW WHO WE
TRULY ARE.

Advocacy is
born of love,
not hate;
of conviction
not blame.

⚖

FAR TOO OFTEN, WE SPEND OUR
LIVES CHASING THE DREAM
WE BELIEVE LIVES OUTSIDE OF
OURSELVES IF ONLY WE COULD
CAPTURE IT. FOREVER JUST OUT OF
REACH, WE EITHER LIVE IN THE PAST
OR MORTGAGE OUR PRESENT BLISS
FOR AN UNKNOWN FUTURE, MISSING
THE BLESSING OF THIS MOMENT
WE ARE NOW IN. WE CLIMB ON
TOWARDS OUR PERSONAL SUMMIT,
FORGETTING THAT WHILE THE VIEW
AT THE TOP MAY BE MAGNIFICENT,
IT IS THE JOURNEY ITSELF & THOSE
WE JOURNEY WITH THAT ULTIMATELY
MAKE THE TRIP WORTH THE WHILE.

"TRENCHES"

IT IS OFTEN WHAT WE 'DO' IN THE
TRENCHES OF LIFE THAT REAPS THE
GREATEST REWARDS. THIS IS WHERE
WE LEARN TO APPLY & REFINE
LIFE'S LESSONS, THOUGH THEY ARE
OFTEN PAINFUL IN THE LEARNING.
WE STRUGGLE IN OUR EFFORTS, &
LEARN TO PERSEVERE. WE START TO
GIVE UP HOPE, BUT THEN LEARN TO
MOVE FORWARD IN FAITH. WE ARE
MET WITH DECEPTION, BUT LEARN
TO COUNTER IT WITH TRANSPARENCY
& INTEGRITY. WE ARE BEATEN DOWN,

& WE LEARN TO STAND UP FOR
OURSELVES. WE FEEL VICTIMIZED,
THEN LEARN TO BECOME OUR OWN
HEROES. WE MOVE IN THE MIDST
OF CHAOS BUT LEARN TO ALIGN
ACTIONABLE GOALS WITH A COMMON
VISION. IN THE FACE OF BLAME,
WE LEARN ACCOUNTABILITY. IN
THE FACE OF FAILURE, WE LEARN
HUMILITY. WHEN CULTURES &
VALUES CLASH, WE LEARN TO FIND
ALIGNMENT WITHIN OURSELVES.

SOMETIMES WE MUST
CLIMB HILLS TO DEVELOP
ENDURANCE OR VISIT
THE VALLEY OF TEARS TO
KNOW COMPASSION, FOR
HOW CAN WE OFFER TO
OTHERS WHAT WE HAVE
NEVER EXPERIENCED FOR
OURSELVES?

🦋

TRUST IS AT THE HEART OF
BUILDING AUTHENTIC CONNECTION
& RELATIONSHIPS WITH OTHERS.
WHEN THE MOTIVES OF ONE ARE
QUESTIONED BY THE OTHER, IT
UNDERMINES ALL POSSIBILITY OF
PROGRESS.

HAPPINESS IS NOT ABOUT GETTING
WHAT YOU WANT, BUT BEING WHO
YOU ARE.

AS YOU GET CLEARER ON WHERE YOU
ARE GOING, IT BECOMES EASIER TO
LET GO OF WHAT YOU MIGHT
LEAVE BEHIND.

IN UNCERTAIN TIMES, WE CAN
CONTROL OUR RESPONSE TO CHANGE
BY HOLDING ONTO OUR VALUES.

THERE IS NO GREATER TRAGEDY
THAN UNEXPRESSED LOVE &
UNREALIZED POTENTIAL.

OUR DREAMS EXPAND OR CONTRACT
IN DIRECT PROPORTION TO OUR OWN
GROWTH & BELIEF OF
WHAT'S POSSIBLE.

WHEN WE TRULY KNOW, HONOR,
TRUST & ACT FROM OUR CORE
SELVES; WHEN WE LEAD FROM
WITHIN, WE EMPOWER OURSELVES &
OTHERS BEYOND MEASURE.

THERE IS A RISK IN RIGHTING
OURSELVES; IN UNCOVERING THOSE
TRUTHS THAT DEFINE OUR LIVES.
THERE IS A RISK THAT IN THE
UNVEILING OF WHO WE TRULY ARE,
WE WILL NO LONGER 'FIT-IN,'
AS DEFINED BY OUR OWN
EXPECTATIONS OR OTHERS'. IN THE
FACE OF THESE TRUTHS, WE RISK
REJECTION, ALIENATION, & CHANGE.
WE RISK UPROOTING OUR LIFE AS
WE ONCE KNEW IT IN EXCHANGE
FOR AN UNCERTAIN OUTCOME,
CERTAIN ONLY THAT IN TAKING THIS
RISK & DOING THE WORK, WE WILL
EVENTUALLY FIND ALIGNMENT &
PEACE WITHIN WHERE THERE ONCE
WAS NONE.

The real adventure in life is not in knowing how the story will end, but in living its unfolding.

❀

WE STRUGGLE IN PROPORTION TO
OUR DESIRE TO RESIST CHANGE;
WE GROW IN PROPORTION TO OUR
WILLINGNESS TO EMBRACE CHANGE.

ON THE OTHER SIDE OF
STRIVING FOR ACCOLADES &
ACCOMPLISHMENTS LIES AN
OPPORTUNITY TO SERVE OTHERS; TO
FIND MEANING & PURPOSE EVEN IN
THE MUNDANE.

THE FIRST & MOST IMPORTANT
DIFFERENCE WE CAN MAKE IN THIS
WORLD IS TO LIVE A LIFE IN WHICH
OUR OUTER LIFE MIRRORS OUR
INNER VALUES.

FAITH SAYS, "I BELIEVE EVEN WHEN I CANNOT SEE, FOR THE DREAM IS ROOTED DEEPLY IN MY HEART."

LOSING, IN A CURIOUS SENSE, CAN ACTUALLY BE A FORM OF WINNING; FOR WHEN WE LOSE THE THINGS WE VALUE MOST; WHEN WE SIT IN THE VOID OF LOSS LONG ENOUGH, THE FEAR BEGINS TO LOSE ITS GRIP. WE START TO SEE THAT WHAT REMAINS IS WHAT EACH OF US AS HUMAN BEINGS DESIRE MOST -- LOVE. NOT LOVE OF A THING OR LOVE FROM A BODY, BUT THE ESSENCE OF OURSELVES, WHICH AT ITS CORE, IS LOVE.

The only person
we can ever
truly know is
ourselves.
♡

LEADERSHIP IS A PRIVILEGE, NOT
AN ENTITLEMENT.

JUDGEMENT – WHETHER OF
OURSELVES OR OTHERS – IS USUALLY
BIRTHED FROM A PLACE OF FEAR,
NOT LOVE; FROM A PLACE OF
REACTION, NOT RESPONSIVENESS;
OR PERHAPS EVEN FROM A PLACE OF
DEEP LACKING WITHIN OURSELVES.

SOMETIMES ALL THAT IS NEEDED TO
CHANGE A LIFE, IS TO CHANGE THE
LENS THROUGH WHICH WE VIEW IT.

IT MATTERS LESS WHERE WE'VE
BEEN, THAN WHERE WE ARE GOING.

WHEN WE GIVE OURSELVES
PERMISSION TO SIMPLY BE; TO SIT IN
THE VOID OF EXTERNAL LABELS OF
SUCCESS; WHEN WE CAN CONNECT
FROM THIS PLACE OF TOTAL HONESTY
& NAKED VULNERABILITY, WE BEGIN
TO DISCOVER THE TRUE MEANING
OF ACCEPTANCE. IT IS IN THIS
ACCEPTANCE OF BEING; IN THIS
ABSENCE OF BOTH JUDGMENT &
ADORNMENT, THAT WE CAN FINALLY
FIND PEACE & JOY.

TAKING OWNERSHIP OF YOUR TRUTH
REQUIRES COURAGE, COMPASSION,
AND ACCOUNTABILITY; IT IS THE
ULTIMATE ACT OF LOVE
& SELF-RESPECT.

THE OPPORTUNITY TO LEAD IS AN
INVITATION TO SERVE
(NOT SELF-SERVE).

THE FUTURE IS MADE UP OF A
THOUSAND PRESENT MOMENTS, SO
LIVE EACH MOMENT TO ITS FULLEST
PURPOSE, WITH COMPASSION,
COURAGE, & INTEGRITY.

AN ATTITUDE OF GRATITUDE CAN
CARRY US THROUGH EVEN THE MOST
CHALLENGING TIMES & OFTEN
OPENS THE DOOR TO NEW PATHS
& POSSIBILITIES.

TO LEAD FROM THE HEART IS AN
ACT OF LOVE.

Our confidence grows in proportion to our core belief about ourselves.

THERE COMES A POINT WHEN IT'S TIME TO STOP LOOKING BACK; WHEN THE EXCAVATION PROCESS ENDS & THE SHEDDING OF SKIN GIVES WAY TO NEW GROWTH.

BELIEVE YOU MATTER, FOR YOU DO. BELIEVE YOU CAN MAKE A DIFFERENCE & YOU WILL.

TRUE EMPOWERMENT IS NOT JUST ABOUT WHAT HAPPENS WITHOUT, BUT WHAT HAPPENS WITHIN.

TRUE COURAGE IS FOUND IN FACING YOUR TRUTH, NOT IN AVOIDING IT.

MOMENTUM BEGINS THE
MOMENT WE SHIFT FROM A
MINDSET OF FEAR TO FAITH &
FROM INSIGHT TO ACTION.

TRUE LEADERSHIP IS NOT MEASURED
BY THE POWER ONE HOLDS, BUT BY
THE POWER ONE GIVES AWAY.

IT IS OUR JOB...INDEED IT IS OUR
RESPONSIBILITY TO MAKE THE MOST
OF THE HAND WE ARE DEALT. IN
LIFE AS IN CARDS, NOT EVERY HAND
DEALT IS EQUAL TO ANOTHER &
SOMETIMES THE DECK MAY APPEAR
TO BE STACKED AGAINST US. BUT
EVERY HAND IS PLAYABLE. IN THE
END, 'WINNING' IS ABOUT LEARNING
TO PLAY THE HAND YOU ARE DEALT
TO THE BEST OF YOUR ABILITY,
RATHER THAN FOLDING AT THE FIRST
GLIMPSE OF STRUGGLE OR SETBACK.

THE MORE WE COME TO
UNDERSTAND OUR DEEPEST SELVES,
THE GREATER OUR CAPACITY TO
BUILD BRIDGES OF UNDERSTANDING
WITH OTHERS.

RESILIENCY IS THE ART OF
REFRAMING TO CREATE NEW
OPENINGS & POSSIBILITIES FOR
PEACE, GROWTH & JOY.

OUR CONFIDENCE GROWS IN
PROPORTION TO OUR BELIEF
ABOUT OURSELVES.

RISK VULNERABILITY.

WHEN WE COURAGEOUSLY CLOSE THE DOOR TO WHAT WE KNOW IS NOT RIGHT, ANOTHER DOOR ALMOST ALWAYS OPENS, THOUGH QUITE OFTEN, THE PAUSE BETWEEN ONE DOOR CLOSING & ANOTHER ONE OPENING REQUIRES A TENACIOUS RESOLVE & COMMITMENT TO OUR DREAMS.

IN TIMES OF CHANGE OR STRUGGLE, WE DO NOT NEED OTHERS' UNDERSTANDING, SO MUCH AS WE NEED THEIR SUPPORT. WE DO NOT NEED OTHERS' JUDGMENT; BUT RATHER, THEIR ACCEPTANCE. WE DO NOT NEED TO BE SPOKEN TO, SO MUCH AS WE NEED TO FEEL HEARD.

THE MORE WE SERVE OTHERS,
THE MORE THE UNIVERSE OPENS
TO US. THE MORE WE SEEK WAYS
IN WHICH TO USE OUR GIFTS FOR
A GREATER GOOD THAN JUST OUR
OWN SELF-PROMOTION, THE MORE
OPPORTUNITY ARISES TO SHARE
THESE GIFTS. IN PLACING THE
NEEDS OF THE WHOLE ABOVE THE
SELF, WE POSITION OURSELVES AS
LEADERS, & THROUGH THOUGHTFUL
LEADERSHIP, WE CREATE OPENINGS
FOR OTHERS TO GROW.

WE THRIVE FROM A MINDSET OF
LOVE. WE SURVIVE FROM A MINDSET
OF FEAR.

READ, WRITE, STRETCH,
GROW, TRAVEL,
CONNECT, TEACH, SERVE,
LEAD, SHARE, HUG,
LAUGH, CRY, SMILE, HAVE
FAITH, BE GRATEFUL.
SAVOR EACH MOMENT.

THREE RULES OF WORK: OUT OF
CLUTTER FIND SIMPLICITY; FROM
DISCORD FIND HARMONY; IN THE
MIDDLE OF DIFFICULTY
LIES OPPORTUNITY.

WHEN WE BECOME ATTACHED
TO THE STORIES WE TELL ABOUT
OURSELVES & OTHERS, WE LOSE OUR
CAPACITY TO STAY OPEN TO WHAT
IS TRUE. WE SUBCONSCIOUSLY SEEK
OUT PEOPLE & SITUATIONS THAT
VALIDATE OUR STORIES, LIVING
FROM A DEFENSIVE, RATHER THAN
AN INQUISITIVE POINT OF VIEW.

TAKING OWNERSHIP OF YOUR
TRUTH INSPIRES & LIGHTS A PATH
FOR OTHERS.

THERE IS NO REAL LEADERSHIP BUT BY FIRST HONORING & LIVING OUR OWN VALUES.

IT IS OFTEN IN THE GRIT OF LIFE THAT WE FIND ITS BEAUTY. MOMENTS OF HOPE, SPRUNG FROM DESPAIR; COMPASSION FROM SUFFERING; OR FORGIVENESS FROM BETRAYAL.

EMPOWERMENT REQUIRES A WILLINGNESS TO LET GO OF OUR NEED TO BE LIKED. WE CANNOT STAND UP FOR OURSELVES & OUR VALUES & PLEASE EVERYONE ELSE AT THE SAME TIME.

WHEN WE LOSE THE OUTER
TRAPPINGS & ADORNMENTS OF
OUR LIFE, BEYOND THE GRIEF &
FEAR LIES AN OPPORTUNITY - AN
OPPORTUNITY TO MOVE FROM
REACTION TO INTENTION; TO
MINDFULLY CHOOSE WHAT & WHO
WE INVITE INTO OUR WORLD. WE
GET A CHANCE TO REWRITE OUR
SCRIPTS. THOUGH WE CANNOT KNOW
OR CONTROL ALL THAT HAPPENS
AROUND OR TO US, WE CAN SHIFT
FROM A MINDSET OF REACTING WITH
FEAR TO ONE OF REFLECTIVELY
RESPONDING FROM A PLACE
OF LOVE.

CONSTRUCTIVE CHANGE IS
PROACTIVE, NOT REACTIVE.
IT IS MINDFUL, DELIBERATE &
INTENTIONAL. IT DOES NOT OCCUR
UNTIL WE ARE WILLING TO LET
GO OF THE PAST, INCLUDING OUR
ATTACHMENT TO OUR WOUNDS.

EGO IS ALWAYS ROOTED IN FEAR,
WHICH WE SHOULD NEVER ALLOW
TO STAND IN THE WAY OF THE LIGHT
OF LOVE.

INSTEAD OF ASKING, "HOW CAN THE
WORLD SERVE ME?" ASK INSTEAD,
"HOW CAN I USE MY GIFTS TO SERVE
THE WORLD?"

WHEN WE PERPETUALLY VALUE
AND ELEVATE CHARISMA OVER
CHARACTER, WE CANNOT BE
SURPRISED BY THE FAILINGS OF
HUMANKIND. AS LONG AS WE REMAIN
A SOCIETY THAT REWARDS TITLE
OVER INFLUENCE & POWER OVER
DEEP PURPOSE, WE WILL NEVER
PRODUCE THE KIND OF COURAGEOUS
LEADERS NEEDED TO ADVANCE OUR
GROWTH, BUILD BRIDGES OF PEACE
AND CARE FOR OUR SOCIETY.

THE PREGNANT PAUSE BETWEEN
OUR PRESENT & DESIRED FUTURE
OUTCOME, PATIENCE TAKES US OUT
OF A PLACE OF REACTIVE FEAR &
INTO A PLACE OF
REFLECTIVE SURRENDER.

LEADING FROM WITHIN IS ABOUT
LIVING & LEADING FROM OUR
HEART PLACE...OUR HEART SPACE.
IT IS ABOUT TRANSPARENCY,
AUTHENTICITY, INTEGRITY, &
HONOR. IT IS ABOUT CONNECTING
WITH OTHERS, JUST AS WE SEEK
TO RECONNECT WITH OURSELVES,
RECOGNIZING THAT WE EACH HAVE
THE BEAUTIFUL, UNIQUE & AMAZING
GIFT OF OURSELVES TO SHARE WITH
THE WORLD.

♡

THE TRUE POWER OF ANY
COMMUNITY OR COLLECTIVE
TO SOLVE COMPLEX PROBLEMS
& INFLUENCE LASTING
CHANGE, BEGINS & ENDS WITH
RELATIONSHIPS & THE TRUE SPIRIT
OF COLLABORATION.

EVERY DAWN IS A NEW
BEGINNING; A CHANCE
TO CHOOSE FAITH OVER
FEAR, LOVE OVER HATE,
JOY OVER SORROW, &
HOPE OVER DESPAIR.

When we dwell
in the past
or live for the
future, we deny
ourselves the gift
of the present.

AT THE 4-WAY INTERSECTION OF
HEART, HEAD, TALENT, & NEED LIES
OUR GREATEST OPPORTUNITY.

LACK OF STAKEHOLDER ALIGNMENT
IS LIKE A TRAFFIC JAM. WHEN WE'RE
GOING IN MISALIGNED DIRECTIONS,
WE'RE SURE TO CRASH & END UP
IN GRIDLOCK.

TRUST SAYS, "YOU CAN REVEAL YOUR
HEART TO ME."

WHEN WE FEEL SECURE IN OUR
CAPABILITIES, WE CAN SHIFT FROM
SELLING TO SOLVING; FROM A
SELF-CENTRIC MINDSET TO ONE OF
SERVING OTHERS.

SOMETIMES IN LIFE YOU ARE
CALLED TO DO THE VERY THING
YOU THOUGHT YOU COULDN'T DO,
EVEN AS YOU MAY HAVE ALWAYS
DREAMED OF DOING IT. YOU START
TO FOLLOW THE CALLING & THEN
YOU PULL AWAY, WHETHER OUT OF
FEAR, LOGIC, PRACTICALITY, OR
CIRCUMSTANCE. IF YOU'RE LUCKY,
THE UNIVERSE DOES NOT TAKE
'NO' FOR AN ANSWER, BUT INSTEAD
COAXES YOU TO DARE TO TRY AGAIN,
& AGAIN, & AGAIN, UNTIL YOU ARE
FINALLY WILLING TO STEP OUT OF
YOUR FEAR & INTO THE MAGIC.

FAITH REQUIRES A WILLINGNESS
TO SURRENDER OUR 'RIGHTNESS'
& NEED TO CONTROL TO A POWER
& INFLUENCE GREATER THAN THE
LIMITATIONS OF OUR OWN MIND. IN
ESSENCE, IT IS THE SURRENDER OF
OUR EGO TO THE DEEP KNOWING OF
OUR HEART.

JUST AS OUR IMPERFECTION &
DIFFERENCES HAVE THE POWER TO
DIVIDE US, SO, TOO, CAN THEY BE
LEVERAGED TO UNITE US. WHEN
WE ALLOW OURSELVES TO SEE OUR
OWN GOOD IN OTHERS OR OTHERS'
SHORTCOMINGS IN OURSELVES, OUR
PERSPECTIVE BEGINS TO CHANGE &
THE CHANCE TO MAKE A DIFFERENT
CHOICE EMERGES.

AUTHENTICITY IS BORN FROM A
WILLINGNESS TO GIVE UP THE
APPROVAL OF OTHERS IN EXCHANGE
FOR ACCEPTANCE & LOVE OF SELF.

SO OFTEN WE SEEK CONFORMITY
IN THE FACE OF LIMITATION;
WE ASSUME CHANGE IS NEITHER
FEASIBLE NOR POSSIBLE, & FROM
THAT PLACE, SEEK TO FEARFULLY
'FIT IT' TO THE STATUS QUO. BUT
WHAT IF INSTEAD OF ACCEPTING
OUR LIMITATIONS, WE LEVERAGED
THEM...ALLOWING THEM TO
CREATIVELY PUSH US INTO NEW
WAYS OF THINKING & BEHAVING;
ALLOWING THEM TO BE THE
CATALYST FOR GROWTH
& INNOVATION?

Walls & barriers
are built
on fear;
boundaries are
born from love.

THERE ARE ANGELS & MIRACLES IN
OUR MIDST. WE MUST SIMPLY OPEN
OUR HEART TO THE POSSIBILITIES.

LEARN TO SURRENDER TO THE
TRUTH OF WHAT IS, WHILE
EMBRACING THE POSSIBILITY OF ALL
THAT IS STILL YET TO BE.

WHEN WE KNOW WHERE WE'RE
GOING, EVERYTHING BECOMES
POSSIBLE.

THE CATERPILLAR'S FULL BEAUTY
& POTENTIAL IS REVEALED ONLY
IN THE AWAKENING FROM ITS OWN
SLEEP.

We become what we imagine and believe is possible.

NO MATTER HOW JUSTIFIED THE
STORY OF OUR STRUGGLE, HOLDING
ON TO IT ONLY HOLDS US BACK.

COURAGE IS THE WILLINGNESS TO
BE SEEN AS WE TRULY ARE. MORE
THAN RIGHT RISK, COURAGE CALLS
US TO STAND NAKED IN OUR TRUTH
& STRONG IN OUR CONVICTIONS.
IN THE FACE OF UNCERTAINTY, IT
SUMMONS STRENGTH; IN THE FACE
OF FEAR, DETERMINATION; YET
ALWAYS IT MOVES STEADFASTLY
FORWARD IN FAITH.

SOMETIMES CALLINGS ARE NOT SO
MUCH ABOUT OUR OWN PLANS, BUT
ABOUT GOD'S PLAN FOR US.

SO OFTEN WE WAIT FOR OTHERS TO GIVE US PERMISSION TO BE WHO WE ARE, AS IF THE TRUTH OF WHO WE ARE ONLY EXISTS IN THE CONTEXT OF ANOTHER'S VALIDATION. WHILE THIS VALIDATION FROM OTHERS CAN BE TRANSFORMATIVE IN NATURE, GIVING US A TEMPORARY SENSE OF CONFIDENCE THAT ENABLES US TO STEP OUT & BEYOND OUR FEAR, IT IS ONLY WHEN WE CAN BEGIN TO LET GO OF OUR DEPENDENCY ON ANOTHER'S APPROVAL THAT WE BEGIN TO KNOW OUR TRUTH WORTH.

DOING WHAT'S RIGHT IS NEVER ABOUT THE 'OTHER' GUY. CORE VALUES ARE ABSOLUTE, NOT RELATIVE TO THE ACTIONS & INTENTIONS OF OTHERS.

WE MUST BE DISCERNING IN WHO WE CAN TRUST & HOW MUCH WE SHARE; NOT ONLY BECAUSE NOT EVERYONE IS WORTHY OF OUR TRUST, BUT BECAUSE WHEN WE INDISCRIMINATELY OVERSHARE WITH MANY, WE ERODE THE POSSIBILITY FOR DEPTH OF CONNECTION WITH ONE.

SO OFTEN OUR DESIRES ARE FOCUSED ON FORM, NOT FUNCTION; ON FUNCTION, BUT NOT PURPOSE.

Noble vision is
not about serving
the ego, but
serving the needs
of our fellow
humanity.

"LEADERSHIP"

TRUE LEADERSHIP IS INCLUSIVE BY
NATURE, BUILDING BRIDGES RATHER
THAN WALLS THROUGH THE GIFT OF
AUTHENTIC CONNECTION.

ROOTED IN RESPECT, IT HOLDS
SPACE TO ACKNOWLEDGE
DIFFERENCE, WHILE REMAINING
ALIGNED TO ITS CORE VISION
& VALUES.

BORN OF INTEGRITY, IT IS
COURAGEOUS IN THOUGHT, WORD
& DEED, WILLING TO TAKE RISKS &
ADVOCATE FOR WHAT IS RIGHT OVER

WHAT IS POPULAR; FOR WHAT IS
TRUE OVER THE CONVENIENT.

PURPOSEFUL IN NATURE, IT IS NOT
DEFINED BY ITS TITLE, BUT BY ITS
ABILITY TO INFLUENCE
POSITIVE CHANGE.

COLLABORATIVE & HUMBLE, THE
BEST LEADERSHIP SERVES, ENABLES
& EMPOWERS OTHERS TO GROW
INTO THEIR BEST SELVES, SEEKING
NOT TO GLORIFY ITSELF, BUT TO
ACKNOWLEDGE & EXALT THE GOOD
OF OTHERS ALONG THE WAY.

WE ARE NEVER THE
SOLE AUTHOR OF OUR
ACCOMPLISHMENTS.
HONOR & ACKNOWLEDGE
THOSE WHO HAVE BEEN A
PART OF YOUR SUCCESS.

FAILURE IS OFTEN HOW WE LEARN
BEST. FEAR & PRIDE ARE WHAT KEEPS
UP FROM THE LESSONS.

THE GREAT GIFT OF AUTHENTICITY
IS THAT WE NO LONGER NEED TO
LIVE IN THE SHADOW OF WHO
WE ARE.

DO YOU CHOOSE TO STAND IN THE
LIGHT OF WHO YOU ARE, OR ARE YOU
CONTENT TO LIVE IN THE SHADOWS
OF YOUR DREAMS?

FEAR CASTRATES THE HEART, WHILE
COURAGE EXPANDS IT.

SOMETIMES WE ALLOW OTHERS
TO PUT US IN A BOX THROUGH
LABELS, TITLES, & CREDENTIALS;
BY ALLOWING OTHER PEOPLE'S
EXPECTATIONS TO CREATE (SELF)-
LIMITING BELIEFS & PERCEPTIONS
ABOUT WHO WE ARE & WHAT WE
ARE CAPABLE OF — MEASURING OUR
INNER WORTH BY OUTER MEANS. AT
OTHER TIMES, OUR BOXES, LINES
& SAND TRAPS ARE BUILT FROM
WITHIN, RE-ENFORCED WITH FEAR &
COVERED WITH PRIDE.

BEFORE YOU CAN DO, YOU MUST
FIRST BELIEVE YOU CAN.

WHEN WE EXERCISE THE COURAGE TO
FACE OUR FEARS, WE CAN BEGIN TO
TAKE STEPS TO WORK THROUGH THEM.
SOMETIMES THE SIMPLE ACT OF
NAMING THEM IS ALL THAT IS NEEDED
TO BEGIN TO MOVE FORWARD.

WHEN WE'RE LIVING ON PURPOSE,
MAKING A 'LIVING' BECOMES
SECONDARY TO MAKING A LIFE. YOU
CAN'T SUSTAIN ONE WITHOUT THE
OTHER, BUT PRIORITIES SHIFT.

HOPE LIES AT THE INTERSECTION
OF LOVE, FAITH & COURAGE.

Fear is only the
image we create
in our mind.
When you feel
afraid, learn
to paint a new
picture.

THE ABILITY TO CONNECT WITH
OTHERS BEGINS WITH DEEP
CONNECTION TO SELF.

OUR 'INNER' WORK IS REFLECTED IN
OUR 'OUTER' WORK. IT IS THE MEANS
& VALUES BY WHICH WE LIVE & LEAD
OTHERS EVERY DAY.

A SPIRIT OF SERVICE IS BORN OF THE
BELIEF THAT WE ARE EACH PART OF A
LARGER WHOLE.

WE STRUGGLE IN PROPORTION TO
OUR DESIRE TO RESIST CHANGE;
WE GROW IN PROPORTION TO OUR
WILLINGNESS TO EMBRACE CHANGE.

OFTEN OUR GREATEST
OPPORTUNITIES ARE BORN OUT OF
OUR BIGGEST STRUGGLES.

FIND YOUR VOICE, LIVE YOUR
DREAMS, SERVE OTHERS & LOVE
THOSE YOU JOURNEY WITH. IN THE
END, THEY ARE THE ONLY THINGS
THAT TRULY MATTER.

AS WE EMPOWER OURSELVES &
OTHERS TO GROW, WE COLLECTIVELY
ACHIEVE MORE THAN WE COULD
EVER DO ALONE.

OTHERS' MISTAKES CREATE AN
EQUAL OPPORTUNITY FOR US TO
LEARN AND GROW.

BOUNDARIES ARE A GREAT ACT
OF SELF-LOVE & RESPECT,
ESSENTIAL FOR BUILDING HEALTHY
RELATIONSHIP WITH OTHERS.

CONNECTING WITH OTHERS
REMINDS US THAT OUR DREAMS
& GOALS ARE BIGGER THAN OUR
INDIVIDUAL SELVES.

FORGIVENESS IS NOT ABOUT
NEGATING OUR WOUNDS, BUT ABOUT
CHOOSING TO MAKE A DIFFERENT
CHOICE FOR OURSELVES; TO LET GO
OF PAST WRONGS TO CREATE SPACE
FOR NEW GROWTH.

THE COURAGE TO STAND UP IS BORN
OF DEEP CONVICTION; FROM THE
CORE BELIEF THAT OUR VALUES &
IDEALS MATTER ENOUGH TO LEAVE
THE COMFORT OF OUR SAFETY TO
DEFEND THEM.

TO LEAD FROM THE HEART IS TO
LIVE IN SERVICE TO OTHERS.

IN THE SHEDDING OF OLD SKINS
OR MASKS THAT ARE WELL WORN,
THERE IS AN INITIAL & OFTEN
PAINFUL VULNERABILITY THAT
ACCOMPANIES IT. IN THIS SPACE,
WE MUST BE CAREFUL TO LIMIT
OUR EXPOSURE TO THOSE PEOPLE &
ELEMENTS THAT DO NOT SUPPORT
OUR OWN JOURNEY.

BEHIND EVERY STORY, LIES A
SERIES OF STORIES THAT SHAPE
& INFLUENCE WHO WE ARE & THE
POTENTIAL OF ALL THAT WE
MIGHT BECOME.

EVEN IN THE DEPTH OF PAIN OR
DESPAIR, OUR STRUGGLES CAN
PROVIDE US WITH CLARITY OF
PURPOSE, VALUE, & PRIORITY.

LEARN TO HONOR THE JOURNEY
ITSELF, FOR THAT IS WHERE TRUE
JOY LIVES.

FIND THE JOY & LESSON IN EACH
MOMENT. IF HARD, PERSEVERE;
IF DESPAIRING, OFFER HOPE; IF
DECEITFUL, ELEVATE TRUTH; IF
HURT, OFFER COMPASSION.

THE MOST IMPORTANT CHOICE WE
MAKE IS ONE THAT IS IN ALIGNMENT
WITH OUR AUTHENTIC CORE.

True humility
in leadership
is essential
to building
communities
of trust.

Honor the deepest truth of who you are.

♡

SEE WITH OPEN EYES. THINK WITH AN OPEN MIND. DREAM WITH AN OPEN HEART.

IT MATTERS LESS THAT WE'VE FALLEN DOWN, THAN HOW WE'RE CHOOSING TO STAND UP.

WHEN WE FAIL TO DEFEND OUR MOST DEEPLY HELD BELIEFS, WE BETRAY OUR CORE SELVES AND VALUES.

THE SUBSTANCE OF VISION IS HARD WORK.

If you don't like what you see, first look in the mirror, then try changing your perspective.

SOMETIMES WE MUST EXPERIENCE
PAINFUL LOSS THAT WE MIGHT
KNOW GRATITUDE, UNCERTAINTY
THAT WE MIGHT KNOW FAITH, &
DISAPPOINTMENT THAT WE MIGHT
KNOW HOPE.

WE LEAD BEST BY EXAMPLE.
TRANSPARENCY IN OUR OWN JOURNEY
OFTEN PROVIDES INSPIRATION &
ENCOURAGEMENT TO OTHERS.

LIVE YOUR VALUES. VALUE YOUR LIFE.

WE EACH WALK OUR OWN PATH, YET
WE ARE ALL A PART OF THE WHOLE.

SEASONED BY TIME & HUMBLED IN HEART, THE BEST LEADERS INSPIRE OTHERS TO GREATNESS, NOT BY WHAT THEY HAVE ACHIEVED, BUT THROUGH THE ESSENCE OF WHO THEY ARE.

TO FIND OUR ANSWERS, WE MUST EMBRACE THE QUESTIONS. TO FIND THE PATH FORWARD, WE MUST FIRST UNDERSTAND THE STRUGGLE ITSELF.

OUR LESSONS ARE UNIQUE TO OUR OWN JOURNEY. OVER TIME, THEY BECOME THE CATALYSTS THAT UNLOCK THE KEY TO OUR VERY SOUL, WITHIN WHICH LIES OUR ESSENCE, PURPOSE, & THE DEEPEST DREAMS OF OUR HEART.

THE DEEPER OUR CONNECTION
WITH OURSELVES, THE GREATER
OUR CAPACITY TO AUTHENTICALLY
CONNECT WITH OTHERS.

FOCUS ON GROWTH INSTEAD OF FEAR
& LEARNING INSTEAD OF FAILURE.

EXTEND A HAND & OPEN YOUR
HEART. THE POWER OF AUTHENTIC
CONNECTION IS PRICELESS.

EXTEND A HAND & OPEN YOUR

PATIENCE IS THE ART OF BEING
STILL; OF LISTENING & CREATING
SPACES FOR OUR HEART & SOUL
TO SPEAK, WHILE INVITING THE
UNIVERSE TO PARTICIPATE IN
THE PROCESS.

SHIFTS AND EXPANSIONS ARE NOT
THE SAME AS LETTING OUR DREAMS
DIE OR BURYING THEM UNDER
LAYERS OF FEAR, COMPROMISE, &
DENIAL. IN THE END, WE EITHER
DIE A SLOW DEATH ALONG WITH
OUR BURIED DREAMS, OR THEY
RISE UP AGAIN WITH A VENGEANCE,
DETERMINED TO HAVE THEIR PLACE
IN THE WORLD.

LETTING GO IS A
NECESSARY PART OF
GROWTH & CREATES ROOM
FOR NEW POSSIBILITIES.

WE LOVE BEST WHEN WE REFLECT
BACK WHAT IS ALREADY IN OUR
HEART & SOUL.

TOO OFTEN WE CHOOSE PRACTICAL
OVER THE PURPOSEFUL, STUCK-NESS
OVER GROWTH, & THE SAFE OVER
THE TRUE.

OFTEN THE PATH WORTHY OF
OUR HIGHEST AND BEST SELVES
REQUIRES TREMENDOUS COURAGE &
SACRIFICE ALONG THE WAY.

THE MORE WE CONNECT WITH
PEOPLE DIFFERENT THAN
OURSELVES, THE BETTER WE CAN
SEE OUR COMMON HUMANITY.

HUMILITY IN LEADERSHIP DOES NOT
EXALT ONESELF OR POSITION ABOVE
OTHERS, BUT SEEKS UNDERSTANDING
IN ALL THINGS, WHILE HOLDING
SPACE FOR OTHERS TO SHINE.

THE BEST WAY TO OVERCOME
SELF-PITY IS TO SERVE OTHERS WITH
A GLAD AND HUMBLE HEART.

ADVOCACY IS BORN AT THE
INTERSECTION OF DEEP CONVICTION,
PURPOSE, & PASSION.

VISION = ((DREAMS OF OUR HEART +
TALENT + PLAN FOR GROWTH) X OUR
CORE VALUES) X FAITH

GETTING UNSTUCK REQUIRES
A WILLINGNESS TO CHOOSE; A
WILLINGNESS TO PICK A PATH
INSTEAD OF STANDING ON THE
SHORES OF UNCERTAINTY OR
AMBIVALENCE.

ONE CANNOT LEAD FROM THE
HEART IF THE HEART IS A STRANGER.
FIRST RULE OF HEART-ALIGNED
LEADERSHIP: KNOW THYSELF.

BE BOLD, TAKE RISKS & ALLOW
YOURSELF TO BECOME A POSSIBILITY
THINKER, ERASING THE LINES OF
LIMITATIONS.

We may never fully know all of the secrets of the universe, but by opening our hearts, we can touch, feel, & taste its wonder.

♡

THE STRENGTH OF OUR OWN
VOICE & TRUTH DOES NOT
DEPEND ON THE APPROVAL OR
VALIDATION OF OTHERS.

♡

CREATIVITY EXTENDS FROM A MINDSET OF POSSIBILITY. IT IS THE BEAUTIFUL EXPRESSION OF OUR MOST AUTHENTIC SELVES.

TO DREAM IS TO PAINT STROKES OF POSSIBILITY ON THE CANVAS OF YOUR LIFE.

PEOPLE PLEASING, PROVING, APPROVAL-SEEKING, & PERFECTIONISM ARE THE FOUR ENEMIES OF PERSONAL PROGRESS.

A GIFT TO OURSELVES & OTHERS, HOPE HELPS PAVE THE PATH TO OUR COLLECTIVE POTENTIAL.

ABOUT THE AUTHOR

Sharon Reed is a blogger, author, advocate, speaker, entrepreneur, and innovative change-agent for good, with a passion for helping others find their authentic voice and realize their leadership potential.

Sharon serves as Founder and Chief Empowerment Officer of the Global Girls Project™, a not-for-profit storytelling platform that elevates the importance of character and core values in the global gender conversation. A former communications consultant and Global Community Champion for the United Nations (UN) Empower Women team, she served as co-architect of the award-winning social media campaign, #iamwoman, and later served as project lead and co-editor of the book, *Voices of Change*, released at UN Headquarters during the 60th session of the Commission on the Status of Women.

Her work has been featured in the Huffington Post, Shriver Report, Women in Foreign Policy, and UN Women, among others. She has also won numerous awards for her service, advocacy and leadership work, including the ATHENA International® Women's Leadership Award and Distinguished Rotarian Award, and was recently named one of Mecklenburg County's 50 Most Influential Women in 2016.

In her spare time, Sharon enjoys writing and creating inspirational art and giftware under the brand, Heart by Design™. She lives in Davidson, NC, with her two children, Michael and Allison.

Contact Info:

Website:	www.sharonereed.me
Twitter:	@sharonereed
LinkedIn:	www.linkedin.com/in/sharonereed